The
Saints Book

Kate Dooley, O.P.

Paulist Press

Nihil Obstat
George M. Keating
Censor Librorum

Imprimatur
Most Reverend Peter L. Gerety, D.D.
Archbishop of Newark

July 22, 1980

Art and Design: Gloria Ortíz

Copyright © 1981 by
The Missionary Society
of St. Paul the Apostle
in the State of New York

Library of Congress
Catalog Card Number: 80-82814

ISBN: 0-8091-6547-3

Published by Paulist Press
545 Island Road, Ramsey, N.J. 07446

Printed and bound in the
United States of America

Contents

Introduction

Who are the Christian saints? We see their names everywhere: the streets where we walk, the cities where we live, the churches, the hospitals, rivers, mountains, dogs, plants, holidays, illnesses, foods. The list could go on and on. Many of us are named for a saint. We are so used to these names that we no longer think about the persons to whom the names originally belonged.

Who are these saints whose names are used in such a variety of ways?

In the Church of the first few centuries, the word "saint" meant all who belonged to the Christian community. St. Paul, in his letters, sent greetings to the saints, believers in Jesus Christ, in Ephesus, Philippi, and Colossae. All Christians were called by God to live as "his holy ones."

As Christians began to suffer for their faith, the term "saint" came to mean a particular group of people, those who were martyrs.

Most of the martyrs belonged to the early Church at the time when the Romans ruled the world. Most Romans did not believe that Jesus was the Son of God. The Romans worshiped many gods, believing that they either gave them favors or punished them. Sometimes the Roman emperor said that he was God and that the people had to worship him. Christians believed that their God was the one true God. Therefore, to them all others were false gods, and they certainly were not going to worship the emperor as God. The Romans tried to make the Christians worship their gods. When the Christians refused, they were put in prison, or tortured, or even killed in a cruel way. Those Christians who were put to death for their belief in Jesus Christ were called martyrs. The Christians turned the graves of martyrs into altars and gathered here to celebrate the Eucharist. Every year on the day of the martyr's death, the Christians remembered the martyr in a special way. It was a day of rejoicing, a feast day, because the martyr had received new life. The names of the martyrs were put on a list.

When the Christians celebrated the Eucharist, they would call upon them by name in prayer. In time, many churches were given their names. Today at our Eucharist, we call to mind these martyrs, and we pray that someday we will belong to the fellowship of the apostles and martyrs and all the saints.

In the early fourth century, when the emperor became a Christian, most of the persecutions stopped, so there were fewer martyrs. The word "saint" then came to mean one who led a holy life. Those who led holy lives were called confessors of the faith. This word, like the word martyr, meant those who witnessed to belief in the Lord Jesus. Many of these confessors were hermits. A hermit usually found a remote place to live so that he would not be distracted by things going on around him. His life could then be one of silence and prayer. He fasted and did penance. Sometimes others would come to join him, resulting in the beginning of a monastery.

Confessors also included those who were great teachers and writers (Doctors of the Church), those who preached the Christian faith in an extraordinary way (bishops and missionaries), and those men and women who proclaimed faith in Jesus through their heroic charity.

In order that a saint may be publicly honored, the approval of the Church is necessary. The person must be canonized. This word, canonization, originally meant putting the person's name on a list or "canon." In the early Church, "canonization" took place when the special holiness or the martyrdom of a person was acknowledged. Later, the bishop of an area gave his approval by allowing a feast day to be celebrated in honor of the saint. In the twelfth century, Pope Alexander III insisted that the Pope's approval was necessary before anyone could be honored as a saint. Gradually, a process of formal canonization came about. Today there are three stages in the process: veneration, beatification and canonization. A very thorough investigation takes place that sometimes can last hundreds of years. First, the name of the person and everything about his or her life is written down and sent to an office in Rome. There must be proof that at least two miracles have been worked by God through this person. There must also be evidence that the person led a Christian life in a heroic way. If all this is found to be true, the person is called "Blessed." Then the process goes into the next stage. There are more investigations and there must be proof of miracles worked by God through this person since he or she was acknowledged as Blessed. One investigator raises as many objections as possible, and all of these have to be disproved. If this happens, then the person is officially recognized as a "saint" in a special ceremony at St. Peter's Basilica in Rome. The saint's name is placed in the calendar of the saints, and a feast day is assigned on which the entire Church will honor this person. Churches may also be dedicated to God in memory of the saint. It is important to remember that there are more saints than those who are canonized. There are many saints whose lives are known only to God and who are honored each year on November 1, the Feast of All Saints. Some of your family may be among them.

When we read the lives of the saints of the early centuries, some of the things they did may seem strange to us today. That is because the world in which we live is very different from the world in which they lived. There were very few books, and so the stories of the saints were told from generation to generation. Some of these stories have become legends. The people of those days believed these stories to be true, but today we can't be sure. Sometimes the people who wrote or spoke of the lives of the saints would tell a story to illustrate their holiness. These stories may not have been meant to be taken as real life happenings but rather as a way to picture something about the saint.

As we read the stories of the saints, we begin to realize that the saints are people who believe so strongly in God's love for them that their only thought is to respond to this love with their entire selves. Saints are all kinds of persons: kings and peasants, clergy, monks and nuns, lay men and women, poor and rich,

married and unmarried, learned and unlearned. What they have in common is what we ask to share with them today: a belief in the Lord Jesus who showed us the Father's love and sent us the Holy Spirit to be among us.

The saints are saints because they have followed the great commandment: Love the Lord your God with your whole heart and soul and love your neighbor as yourself. In each age men and women accepted the invitation of the Holy Spirit to love God with their whole heart. Their love for others had no limit.

The saints lived at a particular time in history and in a particular place. Each had his or her own gifts, talents, failings and faults. The saints grew in the love of Christ. They remind us that we can change and continually grow in our love for God and others.

The saints whose lives we relate in this book were holy because of the holiness of God. They belonged to the Lord Jesus just as we belong to him. When we pray, we pray as part of the Christian community who know God through Jesus, just as the saints did. All of us together are the Church. We ask the intercession of the saints, and they pray for us that one day we may share in this fellowship.

St. Albert the Great

Did you ever watch a caterpillar spin a cocoon and then turn into a bright-colored butterfly? Did you ever see a hummingbird fly backward or look at the ants as they build their cities on sidewalks? If you enjoy the things of nature, you are like St. Albert the Great. He loved to watch something grow or change and to make a record of everything that happened to it.

In 1226, when Albert was twenty years old, he joined the Order of Preachers, the group begun by St. Dominic. Albert became a teacher. One of his students was St. Thomas Aquinas. Albert was happy because he could spend his time studying and writing, teaching and preaching. He had a great knowledge of every field of science of his time. During his lifetime he was able to record part of what he knew in thirty-eight large books.

Albert was also chosen to be the head of all the Dominican priests and sisters in Germany. Thus he had to visit each Dominican house in Germany, and he walked to all of these places. This kept him so busy that he could no longer study and write as much as he would have liked, but he was happy because, most of all, he wanted to serve others in whatever way this needed to be done.

In a few years, he was able to return to teaching. But each time he would begin to teach, something else would happen. First, Pope Alexander IV told him that he wanted him to serve as the bishop of Regensburg in Germany. He obeyed, and then in a few years he returned to teaching. But next, Pope Urban IV ordered him to preach about the Crusades throughout Germany and Bohemia (1263–64). After doing that, he finally was able to resume doing the work he loved. He wrote new books and revised old ones.

Then a sad thing happened. Albert's wonderful memory began to fail. His health became poor and he had to give up teaching. This time it was forever.

Albert had spent his whole life giving honor and glory to God. He gave praise to God in both the work that he loved and in the work he did not love. He praised God in his health and in his weakness. Because of his great learning he is a Doctor of the Church.

St. Albert was born in 1206 and died in 1280.

His feast day is celebrated on November 15.

St. Alphonsus Liguori

St. Alphonsus Liguori was a very successful lawyer in Naples, Italy. After only a few years, he gave up his law practice and joined a group of mission preachers. In 1726 he was ordained a priest. After preaching missions in and around Naples, in 1731 he reorganized a community of sisters, and in 1732 in Scala he organized a group of priests for the purpose of preaching. These men were to preach particularly in the country areas where people had no one to instruct them. This was the beginning of a congregation of priests known as the Redemptorists. The Redemptorists were an association of priests and brothers living in community who preached and strove to be like Christ. Alphonsus said that in their missions the priests should preach in such a way that the people could understand. They were to help the people to know how much God loved them and instruct them that someday after the mission they should return again to the same place for a renewal.

There were many difficulties in the beginning for the Order, but gradually more men came to join the group. Pope Benedict XIV approved their rule in 1749. In 1762, Alphonsus was made the bishop of Sant'Agata dei Gati. He was a kind bishop and served the people well. In 1775 he was allowed to resign because of poor health.

The last years of his life were very sad. The kingdom of Naples in which Alphonsus lived was at war with the other kingdoms in Italy. Alphonsus needed the permission of the government for the society to continue its work of preaching. This meant that the government had to approve the rule. Alphonsus was tricked into signing a document that made the rule very different from the one that the Pope had approved years before. The society was thus divided into two sections. The Pope took the Redemptorist house in his kingdom under his protection and appointed another superior, telling the Redemptorists in Naples that they were no longer an approved society. It was all very confusing, but it meant that Alphonsus was excluded from the society that he himself had begun. Sadly, he died before the two groups were reunited.

Alphonsus always wanted the people to love God. He wrote many pamphlets that helped people to know how to pray better. He is best known for his books for priests. These books helped priests to guide people in making good decisions and choosing the right way to act.

St. Alphonsus Liguori was born in 1696 and died in 1787.
His feast day is celebrated on August 1.

St. Ambrose

St. Ambrose was born in Trier in Germany. He was sent to Rome to study law. While he was practicing law in the Roman courts, he was appointed governor of the area around Milan.

Because he was governor, Ambrose was asked to preside over the election of a new bishop for Milan. There was a great argument over the election. Ambrose went to the church and began to speak to the people. Suddenly they began to call out, "Let Ambrose be bishop!" To his amazement, both sides in the dispute agreed that he should become the bishop. Ambrose did not want to do this. Although his family was Christian, he had not yet been baptized. However, the people insisted, and a few days after his baptism, Ambrose was ordained a priest and consecrated bishop of Milan.

Ambrose gave his share of his family's wealth to the poor and urged others to do the same. As a bishop, Ambrose became famous for his preaching. People came from far away to hear his sermons. One of those who came to listen was St. Augustine.

In the time of Ambrose, there were many people who followed the teachings of a man called Arius. Arius taught that Christ was not God. An early council of Christian churches in the year 325 proclaimed that this doctrine was false and that people who taught it or believed it were in error. One of the Arians was the Empress Justina. She ordered Ambrose to hand over his church to the Arians for the Easter services. Ambrose refused, saying: "A bishop cannot give up the temple of God." The empress sent soldiers to take over the church, but Ambrose's people would not let this happen. As a result there was a big riot, and finally the troops withdrew. However, Justina didn't give up. She had the court order Ambrose to appear before the emperor to debate with the Arian bishop. Ambrose knew that this was a trick to arrest him and put him in prison. Therefore he and his people remained within the church which was surrounded by soldiers. They prayed and sang hymns and psalms. Ambrose preached, telling the people that the emperor is a member of the Church and is not above the Church. Finally the soldiers left and the court dismissed the order.

This was not the only time Ambrose had a dispute with the emperor. When some soldiers were killed in a riot, Emperor Theodosius, for revenge, told his troops to kill everyone in sight. About seven thousand people were murdered. Ambrose announced that unless the emperor did public penance for such a terrible

crime, he would not be allowed to come to the Eucharist and to be part of the Christian Church. When the emperor agreed to do the penance, the people were astounded, for no one ever told an emperor what to do, nor did an emperor ever admit that he was wrong.

St. Ambrose was a man of prayer as well as of action. His writings include catechism lessons to the newly baptized on baptism, confirmation, and the Eucharist. Other writings were the sermons that he preached.

St. Ambrose was born about 339/340 and died in 397.

His feast day is celebrated on December 7.

St. Angela Merici

St. Angela Merici was born in Desenzano, a town on the shores of Lake Garda in Italy. When she was still a child her father died. Within a short time, her mother and sister died also, so Angela went to stay with an uncle in the neighboring town of Salo.

At Salo, Angela came to know the Franciscans. She joined the Third Order which enabled her to wear the habit of the Franciscan Order but to remain in her own home. This group was dedicated to works of charity. Their day was devoted to prayer, visiting the sick and dying, and helping those in need. Each member had a director who would guide that person in his or her life of prayer.

After joining the Third Order, Angela went back to her family home in Desenzano. She took over the management of the property and gave catechism lessons to the children who lived in the towns in the lake area. Several women, influenced by her example, also began to give instructions to the children.

Angela was invited to do similar work in Brescia. In 1494 there was war between Germany and France. Northern Italy became the battlefield for the two countries. The poor city of Brescia was first occupied by one country, then by the other. The city had no peace. The leading families in the cities took sides and made war on each other. Angela often tried to make peace between these families. Because she was successful, she was called upon to settle many of the feuds among the noble families.

Angela longed to make a pilgrimage to the Holy Land. She wanted to make the pilgrimage with the prayer that God would show her how she should serve him. The journey was a difficult one, traveling on horseback, on foot, and by ship. In Venice Angela and her friends joined a larger group of pilgrims. There is a legend that when she reached the island of Crete, she became blind. Her friends wanted to return home, but Angela insisted on continuing the pilgrimage and visiting the shrines, even though she was not able to see them. The legend tells, too, that on the way back, in the same place where she lost her

women to help her with the catechism teaching. Their number increased quickly, and Angela gave the name "The Company of St. Ursula" to the group. The members continued to live at home; they had no habit and took no formal vows. The women were to place themselves under a spiritual director and to always have the approval of the bishop for their work. Angela wrote a rule for the women to follow. The rule had no specific laws; it simply detailed Angela's way of loving God by prayer, fasting, good works, and simplicity of life. She continued to direct the group until her death four years later.

During this time Angela also wrote her testament, a gift to be given to her group after her death. The testament was a summary of her instructions to The Company of St. Ursula during her life. It encouraged the could bring peace to people only if they had in themselves the spirit of love.

After Angela's death the group developed in many ways. Their care for the Christian instruction of the young unmarried girls of Brescia later developed into schools throughout northern Italy and France.

Angela's company was different from other religious groups of her time. Her sisters were not to be enclosed. Their work was to be with the family, educating young women to be Christian wives and mothers. Changing the family would change the society. The Company of St. Ursula developed in other ways after her death. The sisters became responsible for the total education of young girls and not only for their Christian instruction. Schools were started in many of the towns throughout northern Italy and France. Gradually, the group became more like the other Orders of the time. They took formal vows and lived together in community. St. Angela had said to them: "If according to times and needs you should be obliged to make new rules and change certain things, do it with prudence and good advice."

sight, Angela's sight was restored as she knelt in prayer before the crucifix.

Upon her return, she resumed her work at Brescia and, when the war drove her out, at Cremona. When many women and young girls wanted to work with Angela, she began to think of forming a society whose work would be the Christian education of young women. She organized a small group of young group to love God always and said that they

St. Angela Merici was born in 1474 and died in 1540.

Her feast day is celebrated on January 27.

St. Anthony of Padua

St. Anthony of Padua (Italy) was really a native of Portugal. He was born in Lisbon and baptized Ferdinand. He is the patron of travelers, of the poor and of miners, and he is invoked as a helper against fever and against animal diseases and even as the finder of lost objects.

At the age of fifteen, Ferdinand entered the Canons Regular of St. Augustine. He lived a life of prayer and study, acquiring a great knowledge of Holy Scripture. It seemed that his life was settled, but one day, when he was already a priest, he met some Franciscan friars. They were on their way to Morocco to be missionaries. Ferdinand was so impressed by their holiness and zeal to preach Christianity that he too wanted to become a missionary. He left the Canons and joined the Franciscan Order at Olivares, near Coimbra, taking the name of Anthony when he joined the Order.

Anthony was sent to Morocco but became very ill upon his arrival. He was so sick that

it was necessary for him to return to his homeland. However, a very strong wind blew his ship off its course, and the boat was forced to land in Sicily. The Franciscans there took him in. He stayed in a small hermitage, praying, reading the Scriptures and doing menial work.

It is said that his ability as a preacher was discovered accidentally. The story is told that at an ordination, the preacher did not come. On the spur of the moment, Anthony was told to preach, proclaiming whatever the Holy Spirit would direct him to say. Very timidly, Anthony began to speak. Everyone saw right away that he had an extraordinary gift for preaching. After that he took up the work of preaching, and a great many people came to believe in the Lord Jesus through him. St. Francis of Assisi made him the first teacher of theology for the Franciscan Order.

But why is Anthony the finder of lost objects? This devotion has its origins in some legends about St. Anthony.

One day Anthony sadly realized that he was missing his Mass book. The book was precious to him because his mother had given it to him many years before. As he began to pray, someone knocked on the door. It was the man who had taken the book. Shaking with fear and regret, he returned the missal to him. Anthony forgave the man at once.

Another time a very poor woman approached Anthony. She was upset because she could not find the money she had saved. Anthony told her that if she would go home and carefully sweep a certain room in her house, the money would be there. And it was!

In pictures, St. Anthony is shown in many ways: with a book because of his knowledge of Scripture; with a cross because he preached the love of Christ on the cross; with a flame or burning heart because of his great love for God; holding the Christ Child as the sign of his holiness.

St. Anthony was born in 1195 and died in 1231.

His feast day is celebrated on June 13.

St. Augustine

Most mothers worry about their children. St. Augustine's mother did, too—and she had good reason! Born at Tagaste in the Roman province of Africa (now Algeria), Augustine had a pagan father, Patricius, and a Christian mother, St. Monica. Although he was not baptized as a child, he did receive a Christian education. He was very intelligent but did not work in school. Studies did not interest him, only games and sports.

However, his lack of interest in school did not last too long. Augustine began to study hard and became a teacher. He then gave up what little Christian faith he had and joined a religious sect called the Manicheans. He was always restless and moved from thing to thing and place to place. From Africa he went to Rome and then to Milan, in northern Italy. He always seemed to be searching for something.

In Milan, out of curiosity he went to hear the preaching of the bishop, St. Ambrose. These sermons changed Augustine. They answered many of the questions that he had about God and about the Bible. It took him a while to think things through, but in 387 he was baptized.

St. Monica, his mother, had never stopped praying for him and had never stopped loving him no matter what he did. She came to live with him and with great happiness witnessed his profession of faith in the Lord Jesus.

Monica and Augustine prepared to return to Tagaste. At the seaport of Ostia, where they were to get the boat to Africa, Monica died. Her death was a happy one because her son had become a Christian.

Augustine went back to Tagaste, sold the family property and gave the money to the poor. He then started a kind of religious community and spent his days in prayer, silence and study.

Once, when he traveled into Hippo, a group of people insisted that he become a priest to help their bishop and to serve in their city. With reluctance, Augustine was ordained a priest. Then when the bishop of Hippo died, Augustine became the bishop.

From then on, Augustine devoted his whole life to preaching and teaching the kingdom of God. He wanted to make up for all the years that he had wasted, all the years in which he had not loved the Lord Jesus. He said, "How late have I loved you!"

He preached every day and wrote a large number of books against the false beliefs held by many people of that time. Among these people were his former friends, the Manicheans. He wanted to make the truth known. He also wrote his *Confessions,* a beautiful book, in which he thanks God for having loved him and for having called him to serve him. The *Confessions* tell the story of Augustine's search for God. Augustine said, "You have made us for yourself, O Lord, and our hearts are restless until they rest in you."

His writings have had great influence in the Church in every period of history. Augustine was very wise and was named a Doctor of the Church.

St. Augustine was born in 354 and died in 430.

His feast day is celebrated on August 28.

St. Augustine of Canterbury

Augustine was the prior of St. Andrew's Monastery in Rome. With about forty other monks, Pope Gregory I sent him to England to preach the Christian faith. Venerable Bede tells us the story of Augustine in his *History of the English Church and People*.

The missionaries needed a lot of courage because they had heard dreadful stories about the difficult sea voyage. Even more frightening were the stories of the cruelty and savageness of the people they were going to serve. Furthermore, they didn't even know the language of these people. When they got to the coast of France, where they were to begin their sea journey to England, they decided not to go on. They wanted to return to Rome to ask the Pope to let them give up this dangerous journey, and they persuaded Augustine to go back to make this request for them. Augustine did so, but Pope Gregory told him not to be afraid. The Pope sent a letter to the others urging them to continue and to complete this great work of preaching God's Word. Although they were still afraid, they went on.

When they arrived in England, the monks went to Ethelbert, the most powerful king in the country at that time. The king had heard of the Christian religion, and he told them that their teachings were new and uncertain. He said, "I cannot accept them and abandon the old beliefs that my people have always held." Nevertheless, he gave them permission to preach. He even gave them a place to stay in the city of Canterbury. The monks went to this house. They spent their time in prayer, they fasted and did penance, and they accepted only what was absolutely necessary for them in order to live. They preached the Word of God to everyone who would listen. The monks practiced what they preached. They were willing to endure any hardship. They were even willing to die for the truths they taught. Their humble, simple lives were admired by the people. Before long many people came to believe and were baptized. Even the king was baptized.

In Canterbury, on the ruins of a pagan temple, Augustine built a church that today is called the Cathedral of Canterbury. Near the church he built a monastery. After he was consecrated a bishop in Arles, France, he made Canterbury the center of his territory.

Augustine didn't always meet with success. Some of the Christians were faithful to the practices taught by St. Columban and the other Irish/Scottish missionaries who had different customs from those of the Church in Rome. For example, they had a different date for Easter. This meant that some parts of the country would celebrate Easter two or three weeks earlier than others. They also had different ways of baptizing. This caused confusion among the people. Augustine tried to meet with the leaders of the Irish Church and to get them to change over to the practice of Rome. The meeting was a failure, and the conflict was not settled until after Augustine's death.

Augustine died after only seven years in England, but he accomplished a lot in a short time. He brought Christianity to England and established churches and monasteries. He was buried in the Cathedral of Canterbury.

St. Augustine died in 604.
His feast day is celebrated on May 27.

St. Barnabas

We read about St. Barnabas in the Acts of the Apostles in the New Testament.

"There was a certain Levite from Cyprus named Joseph, to whom the apostles gave the name Barnabas (meaning Son of Encouragement). He sold a farm that he owned and made a donation of the money, laying it at the apostles' feet" (Acts 4:36–37).

In the Acts we learn that Barnabas brought St. Paul to the other apostles and convinced them to accept him. He assured the apostles that Paul was no longer their enemy (Acts 9:27).

Barnabas was chosen to go with Paul on a missionary journey to the island of Cyprus to bring the Gospel to the people. Barnabas and Paul traveled over the island teaching the people about Jesus. They had many difficulties. At one place the people threw stones at Paul, dragged him out of the town and left him to die. Barnabas and his other friends cared for Paul and Paul got up and went right back into the town. Despite their dangers and hardships, many people did come to believe in the Lord Jesus through their witness.

Barnabas and Paul finished their missionary journey and went to Jerusalem for a meeting of the leaders of the Church (Acts 15:2–29). There was a controversy among the leaders. Some said that the Christians who had not been Jews first should obey the Jewish laws also. Barnabas and Paul argued that these Christians should not be made to do that. After much discussion, the assembly agreed with Barnabas and Paul.

The leaders decided to send Barnabas and Paul to Antioch, in Syria. The leaders wrote a letter to encourage the Church at Antioch. Barnabas and Paul were to carry this letter to them. Paul and Barnabas, with other apostles, taught and preached the Word of the Lord in Antioch. After a time, Paul suggested that they go back to the towns where they had first preached. Barnabas wanted to take along his cousin, John Mark. Paul objected because John Mark had gone with them the first time and had deserted them on the way. Paul said that John Mark was not fit to go along with them. The disagreement was so sharp that the two men separated. Barnabas and John Mark went to Cyprus. Paul and Silas traveled throughout Syria and Cilicia. (Many years later, John Mark did become a worker with Paul and was praised by him.)

According to a legend, Barnabas was martyred in Cyprus. The legend also tells that when Barnabas' body was found, he had a handwritten copy of St. Matthew's Gospel over his heart. Because of this story, the pictures of St. Barnabas often show him carrying a Bible in his hand along with the staff of an apostle. "He was a good man filled with the Holy Spirit and faith" (Acts 11:24).

St. Barnabas lived during the first century.

His feast day is celebrated on June 11.

St. Benedict

St. Benedict was born at Nursia in Italy. When he was a young man, his father sent him to study in Rome. During that time Benedict knew that God was calling him to the life of a monk. Benedict went to live in a cave near a little town called Subiaco. He remained there for three years, living in silence, prayer and penance. Soon others came to ask if they could share his life. Gradually the group grew larger and larger. Benedict began to build houses in various places where these groups of men who wanted to become monks could live. About the year 529, Benedict started the famous monastery of Monte Cassino.

Benedict helped his followers to live a holy life by giving them a rule. The rule was a book that told the monks the ways in which they could best live together to love God. Benedict used the Bible and the writings of holy persons as helps in writing the rule.

Benedict said that the monastery (the house where the monks lived) was a school for the service of the Lord. A monk called an abbot would be the head of the monastery. The monks would spend their day praising God by praying together, doing spiritual reading, and sharing in the manual work. The monks would share everything they had.

Benedict died at Monte Cassino and was buried there with his sister, Saint Scholastica.

Little by little, the Rule of St. Benedict spread throughout western Europe. Today there are many men and women all over the world who call themselves Benedictines because they try to love God in the way shown to them by St. Benedict in his life and his rule.

The monastery of Monte Cassino has been destroyed and rebuilt three times. Invading tribes destroyed the monastery in the year 600 and again in 900. It was also ruined during World War II. Today it is again rebuilt and stands in memory of St. Benedict's life and work. In 1964, Pope Paul VI named St. Benedict the patron saint of Europe.

The motto of the Benedictine Order is Ora et Labora—Pray and Work. "You should prefer absolutely nothing to the love of Christ, who will lead us all together to eternal life" (CH 72, Rule of St. Benedict).

St. Benedict was born about the year 480 and died around 547.

His feast day is celebrated on July 11.

St. Bernard of Clairvaux

St. Bernard of Clairvaux was born near Dijon in France. When he was about twenty-one years old, he joined a very strict order of monks at the monastery of Citeaux. His family was disappointed because the monastery was very poor and the monks were old. In fact the monks knew it would not be long before the monastery would have to close because no young men were coming to join them. Imagine their amazement when not only Bernard entered their monastery but also his brothers and over twenty of his friends.

The monastery grew so quickly that in three years Bernard was sent to open another monastery at Clairvaux. It was a wild, wooded valley and the monks built a crude shelter there for a house. They had not been able to clear the land to grow crops before winter began. It was very cold and they did not have enough to eat. The monks wanted to go back to Citeaux. Bernard begged them to stay and said that God would help them. A nearby monastery heard of their difficulties and sent them food to last through the winter. After this hard beginning, the monastery grew. Many men came to join them. Their life was very strict. They spent long hours in prayer and silence, did hard work on the farm, fasted, and had very little sleep.

Bernard's holiness and learning became widely known. Many times he was called upon to settle disputes. He was a gentle man but fearless in giving his opinions, never hesitating to correct even kings and nobles if he thought they were wrong. In 1130 when Pope Honorius II died, Pope Innocent II was elected as his successor. A rival group elected another man, Anacletus II, and said that he was the Pope. Bernard left his abbey and went to help

Pope Innocent. Bernard also went to the king of England, to the German emperor and to everyone else who might be able to help. Because of his holiness and because of his ability to speak to them so well, Bernard was successful. Pope Innocent returned to Rome as the legitimate Pope.

Bernard had to leave the monastery many times to help others. Pope Eugene III asked him to preach a Crusade. A Crusade was sometimes called a holy war. Its purpose was to regain the city of Jerusalem from the Turks who had captured the city and were persecuting the Christians. Bernard obeyed and preached in France and in Germany about the holiness and the justice of such a war. Because of his preaching, thousands of men joined the Crusade. However, the ideals of the men and some of their leaders were not always those of Bernard. The men marched across Europe in a disorderly way. Many of them became ill and died on the way. Those who reached Asia were either killed or taken prisoner. The Crusade was a terrible failure. Bernard did not know that the Crusades were a mistake from the beginning. He was saddened by the whole event. After the failure, Bernard felt that he had to bear some of the blame. This was a heavy burden.

With all these activities and despite poor health, Bernard nevertheless wrote many books. Some of them were sermons for his monks; others were sermons on the love of God. Many of his wriitings were so outstanding that he was named a Doctor of the Church. Pope Pius VIII called him a honey-sweet teacher, and so he has a beehive as his emblem.

In 1153, worn out from work and from penitential practices, Bernard died. The monastery at Clairvaux was his monastery, but during his lifetime he founded sixty-eight others. Today there are Cistercian monasteries throughout the whole world where monks try to live the ideals that Bernard taught so well.

St. Bernard was born about 1090 and died in 1153.
His feast day is celebrated on August 20.

St. Blase

It is the custom on the feast of St. Blase to have the blessing of throats. The priest holds two crossed candles at the throat of the person and prays: "Through the intercession of St. Blase, bishop and martyr, may God deliver you from all ailments of the throat and from every other evil. In the name of the Father, and of the Son, and of the Holy Spirit."

This blessing does not mean one will never again have a sore throat. Rather, it is a prayer that members of the Church make for each other. It reminds us that good health is a blessing and that we should pray for one another.

This blessing, begun in the sixteenth century, has its origin in the legend that St. Blase once saved a small boy from choking to death on a fishbone caught in his throat. At Blase's command, the child coughed up the bone and was able to breathe once again.

Most of what is known about Blase has come to us through legend because there was nothing written down about him when he was alive. It is believed that he was the bishop of Sebaste in Armenia in the late third century. Because the persecution of the Christians still continued, Blase's friends hid him in a cave so that he would not be put to death. There he lived as a hermit in silence and prayer. One story relates that Blase made friends with all the wild animals. A group of hunters accidentally discovered Blase's cave and found him kneeling in prayer, with the wolves, lions, and bears all clustered around him, patiently waiting for him to finish. The hunters dragged Blase off to prison. When he refused to worship the false gods, he was put to death.

It is not known when St. Blase was born but he is thought to have died about the year 316.

His feast day is celebrated on February 3.

St. Bridget of Sweden

St. Bridget was the daughter of a wealthy landowner. She married Ulf Gudmarsson and they had eight children. Their second child was St. Catherine of Sweden.

Bridget lived most of her married life at the court of the Swedish king, Magnus II, where she was the principal lady-in-waiting to Queen Blanche. Bridget tried hard to help the king and queen to take their duties to their people seriously, but they did not pay much attention to her.

When her husband died, Bridget began to live a life of prayer and penance, and she re-ceived money from King Magnus to build a monastery for monks and nuns. The two houses of the monastery were joined by a church, where both groups came to pray. The head of the nuns, the abbess, was in charge of both groups. Eventually this order became known as the Order of the Holy Savior or Bridgettines. The monks and nuns could have no possessions of their own except books. Each religious could have as many books for study as he or she wished. Every year, any money that was left over was given to the poor. Their day was spent in prayer, study and work.

In 1350 Bridget made a journey to Rome to ask the Pope for approval of her Order, and she never returned to Sweden. In Rome, she lived very poorly, looking after the sick and the poor and giving very frank advice to the Pope about the serious problems of the times. She also tried to reform some of the monasteries in the area. Her daughter, St. Catherine, came to Rome to be with her and share in her work.

Bridget made many journeys to the shrines of saints in Italy. Her last pilgrimage was to the Holy Land. In each place she visited on her journey, she tried to warn the people, begging them to change their sinful way of living. She met with much opposition because people did not want to hear the truth. On her return to Rome, she became ill and died there.

Today there are only a few Bridgettine convents (these are now only for nuns) that trace their beginnings to St. Bridget. However, new houses of the old Order have been founded in various parts of the world.

Bridget wrote a book in which she told the things that had been revealed to her about our Lord and about future events. These writings show that her prayer impelled her to action. Her prayer was not separate from the rest of her life, but rather her prayer showed her what she must do.

St. Bridget of Sweden was born about the year 1303 and died in 1373.

Her feast day is celebrated on July 23.

St. Boniface

St. Boniface was baptized Winfrid, but he has always been known as Boniface. Until he was about forty years old, Boniface was a Benedictine monk and was also the director of the monastery school in Nursling, England. He longed to bring the Gospel to pagan tribes. Under the direction of St. Willibrord, he went to Frisia, the area around what is now Holland, but the wars in that country forced him to return to England. In 718 he went to Rome to ask the Pope to give to him a mission territory. It was Pope Gregory II who gave him the name of Boniface—"he who does good"—and sent him to preach about Jesus Christ among the Germanic tribes.

Boniface went first to Thuringia in eastern Germany. The area was mostly pagan, although missionaries had been in the area. Boniface preached to the leaders of the people and tried to reform the clergy, most of whom were not very well instructed in the Christian faith. He went again into Frisia and then to Hesse in southwest Germany. He brought the Christian faith to the pagans not only through his words but also through his actions.

Boniface then returned to Rome to inform the Pope about his activities. The Pope made him a bishop and gave him letters to recommend him to the rulers of the German peoples. Boniface took his letters first to Charles Martel, one of the most powerful of the German leaders. Charles Martel gave him a letter of safe conduct which allowed him to travel through Germany without being harmed. This helped his missionary work very much.

A wonderful story is told about how Boniface won over a savage tribe. This tribe worshiped a god of thunder and met for sacrifice around an ancient oak tree that they believed was sacred to the god. When Boniface started to chop down the tree, the tribe was horrified, for they felt sure that the god of thunder would punish them. Boniface continued to chop away, and suddenly there was a terrible crash as the tree fell to the ground. The tribe ran back in fear because they thought that the noise was the god of thunder striking Boniface dead. When they dared to look up, there was Boniface smiling, standing in the sunshine that had been kept away by the great tree. The tribe then came to the conclusion that the God of the Christians must be more powerful than their god, so they began to listen to Boniface and the other monks.

The story tells, too, that Boniface built a small chapel out of the wood of the oak tree. We don't know if this story is really true, but we do know for certain that because of Boniface many tribes came to believe in Jesus Christ. He traveled all through Germany, teaching, preaching, building churches and schools, and establishing convents and monasteries. Monks and nuns from England came to help him. He organized the whole German Church into dioceses and worked especially to unite that Church under the Pope.

By now Boniface was old and frail, and he wanted to return to Frisia, but his desire to spread the Gospel carried him on. At first, all went well, and many came to him to learn the teachings of Jesus. As he was preparing one day to give the sacrament of confirmation to a group of newly-baptized persons a group of pagans attacked them. Thus Boniface died the way he had lived: as a witness to the Lord Jesus Christ. His body was brought back to his monastery at Fulda.

St. Boniface was born about 675 and died in 754 or 755.

His feast day is celebrated on June 5.

St. Casimir

St. Casimir was a prince, the son of King Casimir IV of Poland. His tutor was John Dlugosz, the great Polish historian. Because Casimir was a prince, he could have done anything he wanted, but from his tutor he learned that the important thing in life was to live as a good Christian. Casimir spent time in prayer, did penance, and decided to serve God with his whole heart and soul.

Some of the nobles in Hungary were unhappy with their king, and they asked King Casimir to send his son to take over the country. Casimir obeyed, only to find that his army was outnumbered, some of his troops were deserting, and the battle would result in a needless waste of lives since it was doomed to failure. Thus he returned home. His father was angry and punished him, but the boy continued to pray and to study. He took charge of the kingdom while his father was on tour in Lithuania, but he knew that he never wanted to be king.

Casimir was only twenty-six years old when he died. Renowned for his prayerfulness and for his devotion to the Blessed Mother, he was buried in the cathedral at Vilna, Lithuania. After his death, many miracles were attributed to him, and he was canonized in 1521.

Casimir is the patron saint of Poland and Lithuania, countries that have remained strong in their faith despite great oppression and persecution. He is represented in pictures as holding a banner on which the words of the hymn "Omni die, dic Mariae" are written. We have come to know this hymn as "Daily, daily, sing to Mary." This hymn is called the hymn of St. Casimir because he wanted to have a copy of it buried with him.

St. Casimir was born in 1458 and died in 1484.

His feast day is celebrated on March 4.

St. Catherine of Siena

Can you imagine what it must be like to have twenty-two brothers and sisters? Well, St. Catherine of Siena was the youngest of twenty-three children. In her household there was always laughter and someone with whom to play games.

As Catherine grew up, she was somewhat of a problem for her mother. She refused to be married and she refused to become a nun. When she was still a teenager she joined the Third Order of St. Dominic. The rules of this group allowed her to wear the black and white habit of the Dominican Order but to live in her own home.

For several years, the fun-loving Catherine left her room only to go to Mass in the nearby church. She spent her time in prayer, and she slept and ate very little. Through her prayer she came to realize that God wanted her to work in a special way. She began to nurse the sick, help the poor and visit the prisoners. Soon a group of people began to gather around her and to do the things that she did. They too worked to help those in need. The word of Catherine's holiness spread to other towns besides Siena. Because she was so wise, many people came to her for advice, especially in the settling of feuds and disputes.

There was a serious situation in the Church at this time. When Frenchmen were elected as Pope, they didn't stay in Rome like the other Popes but instead went to Avignon in France. Many of the Popes took orders from the French kings. This made other countries angry. It was not good for the Church either. The leaders of the republic of Florence asked Catherine to go to Avignon to convince the Pope to return to Rome so that there could be peace. Catherine went but it was very difficult. People made fun of her. Some bishops thought that she was giving the people false teachings. They asked her questions over and over again.

Because of her holiness, Pope Gregory XI listened to her and returned to Rome. However, he died within a year. The new Pope, Urban VI, wanted a reform and upset many people. Some of the French bishops said that they had elected him Pope because they were so afraid of the mobs outside who wanted an Italian Pope. Therefore they said that the election didn't count because they had elected him out of fear. These bishops elected another Pope, and this Pope lived in Avignon. It was very confusing and a time of great trial for the Church. Pope Urban VI asked Catherine to help settle this serious dispute.

Catherine knew that she did not have long to live, and she wanted her followers to have her spiritual teachings as her last gift to them. She therefore asked her friends to listen carefully and write down all that she said when she went into ecstasy. During these times of ecstasy, Catherine's body would become stiff and without feeling. She could neither see nor hear. Sometimes she would speak and then others could know the conversation she had with the Lord. She wanted to share this with her followers. The secretaries wrote this down. The book, known as *The Dialogue,* recorded the conversation of the Lord with Catherine.

When Catherine went to Rome, she prayed and fasted that the Church would again be united, and she pleaded with the cardinals and kings to accept Urban VI as the true Pope. Then, in poor health and saddened by the situation around her, she became ill and died in Rome. She had always lived the ideals of St. Dominic in her love for the Church. She, with St. Francis, is the patron saint of Italy. She was made a Doctor of the Church in 1970.

St. Catherine of Siena was born about 1347 and died in 1380.
Her feast day is celebrated on April 30.

St. Clare of Assisi

In Assisi, in the crypt of the small, simple church of Santa Chiara, St. Clare is buried. A sister is there, and her work is to tell all the visitors about the life of St. Clare. This sister is a member of the Order which St. Clare began hundreds of years ago, and she tells this story:

Clare was born to a wealthy family in Assisi. When she was about eighteen years old, she heard a sermon preached by St. Francis of Assisi and she decided to live a life of poverty as Francis did. Francis helped her to leave her home without her family knowing about it. She went to stay at a Benedictine convent. Her father and uncles were very angry and tried to make her come home, but she would not do so. In a few weeks, her sister Agnes came to live in that same convent, and gradually other women joined them. (Later her widowed mother and another sister also joined her.)

Francis took them back to St. Damian near Assisi, where he directed the little group in their life of poverty and prayer. This was the beginning of the Order now called the "Poor Clares." Francis made Clare the abbess in 1215. The nuns went barefoot, slept on the floor, ate no meat, kept almost complete silence and remained always within the convent walls. They owned no property and lived on what people generously gave to them. If there was nothing, then they went without. They spent many hours in prayer. Francis remained Clare's good friend and helped her to love God.

Clare served the sisters and the poor who came for help. For many years of her life she was almost always sick and had to remain in bed. She suffered very much before her death in Assisi, but she accepted this as one more way in which to love God.

St. Clare is often pictured holding a monstrance in her hands. In 1240–41, the Saracens were about to attack Assisi. The Saracens were a tribe who invaded cities, looted, and then often burned the entire city. The story is told that Clare placed the monstrance with the Blessed Sacrament on the walls of the convent, and that then she and the nuns prayed for God's protection. The Saracens turned away and the city was saved. Sometimes pictures of Clare also show her holding a book containing the rule of the Poor Clares (the way of life the nuns followed), a lily (the sign of her love for God), or a crucifix.

St. Clare was born in 1194 and died in 1253.

Her feast day is celebrated on August 11.

St. Dominic

According to a legend, St. Dominic had a dream in which he saw the Blessed Mother presenting two men to her Son. One of them was Dominic himself. The other one he did not know. On the following day, Dominic saw the man whom he had seen in his dream. He ran to him and said, "My brother, we will walk together. Let us hold together and none can overcome us." The other man was St. Francis of Assisi. God had called these two great saints to renew the Church of their age, and, through their followers, the Church of every age.

Dominic was born in Spain in the province of Castile. He was a very good student at the University of Palencia. After becoming a priest, he joined the priests, called canons, who lived at the cathedral in Osma. These priests lived together and owned everything in common. They celebrated Mass, prayed, and gave generously of what they had. They followed the Rule of St. Augustine, living simply and poorly. Dominic became the head of the community. In 1203 he went with his bishop to preach against a group called Albigensians (from the town of Albi in France) who were teaching false doctrines. They talked to the leaders of the Albigensians and to the people who believed these teachings.

In 1206 Dominic founded an institute for women in Prouille where his community was now located. Their work was to pray for the success of the preaching and to help women who were converts from the Albigensians.

Eventually Pope Innocent III began a Crusade against the Albigensians. During these years of turmoil, Dominic and his few followers continued to preach, often with danger to their life.

In 1215, Dominic founded a religious house at Toulouse for his community of friar preachers. This was the beginning of the Dominican Order. These preachers were to live together in community, being of one heart and soul in God, and to share everything in common and to teach and preach anywhere and everywhere. Their life of preaching and teaching was to be based on their life of prayer and study.

In 1216 Pope Honorius II approved the Order, although, like the Franciscans, it was very different from any religious group existing at that time. Friars (from the French word meaning "brothers") did not vow to remain in the same monastery for their entire life.

Dominic spent the next years in organizing the Order, establishing new houses of friar preachers, and traveling and preaching all over Italy, in Spain, and in Paris. Dominic's Order grew quickly. In addition he established an Order of nuns in Rome before dying in Bologna.

In art, St. Dominic is often shown with a dog who carries a flaming torch in his mouth. This symbol has its origin in a dream that Dominic's mother had before he was born. In her dream she saw a running dog with a torch in his mouth setting fire to everything on his way. This dream told the mother that the work of her son was to bring the love of God to all the earth. The Dominicans became known as "The Watchdogs of the Lord" because they protected the Church from error and evil just as watchdogs protect their owners from harm.

Dominic is shown too with a star on his forehead. This is a symbolic way of saying that Dominic shines in the Church like a star in the heavens. The greatness of this saint has been one of the glories of the Church.

St. Dominic was born in 1170 and died in 1221.

His feast day is celebrated on August 8.

St. Elizabeth of Hungary

St. Elizabeth was a princess, the daughter of King Andrew II of Hungary. When she was fourteen, she was given in marriage to Louis II who was the count of an area of Germany called Thuringia. Louis and Elizabeth were very happy, and they had three children.

Elizabeth was a truly Christian woman. She spent her time visiting and nursing the sick and taking food and clothing to the poor. She turned a big house near her castle into a hospital for children and other sick people. She visited there often, bringing little gifts for the patients and helping to care for the children.

There is a lovely legend told about Elizabeth. During the winter, her husband and some of his friends were returning from a hunting trip when they met Elizabeth. Under her cape she was carrying loaves of bread for a poor family. When she saw Louis and the other nobles, she greeted them and tried to hurry by. She did not want them to see the loaves for the hungry family because it was not the custom for rich people to associate with poor people. Elizabeth knew that these men had already made fun of her for helping the poor. They also tried to embarrass her husband, because he always defended Elizabeth whom he loved for her goodness. Louis asked her what she was carrying, and, on an impulse, Elizabeth said, "Roses." At that moment the wind blew Elizabeth's cape open and, to everyone's amazement, out fell beautiful, fragrant roses. The people told this story in order to show that Elizabeth's kindness and generosity to the poor was very pleasing to God.

Those were happy years for Elizabeth, but soon she was to know great sorrow. Louis was asked to join the Crusades. He did not want to leave his family, but he felt that it was his duty to go. However, he died before he ever reached the Holy Land.

Louis' brothers were not as kind as Louis had been. They complained that Elizabeth was giving all their money away, and they

forced her and her daughters out of the castle. Elizabeth had nowhere to go. Often she and her children slept in sheds or barns and begged for their food.

After the Crusades, Louis' friends came back and they made his brothers take care of Elizabeth. Elizabeth settled in the town of Marburg, where she again resumed nursing the sick and helping the poor until her death.

A few years after her death, construction was begun on the beautiful church of St. Elizabeth in Marburg. Visitors from all over the world go there to pray at her shrine. Parts of the frescoes painted in the fourteenth and fifteenth centuries still remain. They tell the story of her life. On her casket, lovely engravings in gold also tell that story which was truly one of service and love of God.

St. Elizabeth was born in 1207 and died in 1231.

Her feast day is celebrated on November 17.

St. Elizabeth Seton

Two hundred years may seem like a very long time. The United States is just a little over two hundred years old as a country, but in comparison to many other countries of the world, this is a very short time indeed. That is one reason why, in 1975, there was such special joy in the United States when Elizabeth Ann Seton was canonized a saint by the Church. She was the first person born in that country to be declared a saint.

Elizabeth was born just before the American Revolution. Her mother died when she was three years old. Although her father married again, Elizabeth and her sister spent most of their time with their uncle in New Rochelle, N.Y. When Elizabeth was eighteen, she married William Seton. They had five children: Anna Maria, Rebecca, Bill, Dick and Kit. They were a very happy family until Mr. Seton became ill in 1803.

Elizabeth and her husband thought that a warmer climate would be good for his health. With their eight-year-old daughter, Anna, they sailed from New York to Italy, where they had friends. When they arrived in Italy they were told that because of a yellow fever epidemic in New York they would have to remain in quarantine for one month. The hospital was not like the ones we know today. Their room, which had a brick floor and only a bench to lie on, was very cold and damp. Mr. Seton became even more ill. Finally they were released, but he died within a few weeks.

The people with whom Elizabeth stayed were very kind to her. Through them she came to know about the Catholic Church. When she returned to New York, she decided to become a Catholic. Catholics in Elizabeth's time were often poor and many did not know how to read. Elizabeth's family thought that Catholics were lower class, lazy, and ignorant. When she said that she was going to become a Catholic, her family was very angry, and they all turned against her.

Elizabeth had to find a way to take care of her children. That was very difficult, since her family and friends had rejected her. She finally decided to open a boarding school for young children. At the same time she began to go to St. Peter's Church, which was then the only Catholic church in New York City. In 1805 she made her profession of faith and was received into the Catholic Church.

The following year, while at church, she met a priest who encouraged her to come to Baltimore and open a boarding school there for Catholic girls. There was no school for Catholic girls in the United States at that time. Elizabeth went to Baltimore, and other women who shared her faith and ideals came to join her. The school grew and soon another building was needed. Elizabeth was given money to buy a farm in Emmitsburg, Maryland for a school.

In 1808 Elizabeth made private vows to Archbishop John Carroll of Baltimore. After her husband's death she had thought often of joining a religious order but she had to care for her family. Now she took the vows that sisters profess, even though she was not a member of a religious order. Instead, she was to begin one!

The other women who helped her with the school also wanted to be sisters. In 1812 Elizabeth and the others made formal vows. They were called the Daughters of Charity of St. Vincent de Paul. Elizabeth became the head of this community of sisters, and from that time on she was known as Mother Seton.

During these years, Elizabeth knew much sorrow. Her husband's sisters, Cecilia and Harriet, had both become Catholics and had come to Baltimore to join her. Sadly, both of them died shortly after their arrival in Baltimore. The following year, 1812, Elizabeth's daughter Ann also died. Four years later, Becky died. Elizabeth knew that she herself was ill and would not have long to live.

Mother Seton began the first Catholic school for girls in the United States and founded the first native religious community. Her sisters now serve in hospitals, schools, orphanages, homes for the aged, and homes for

St. Francis of Assisi

The city of Assisi, built of pink stone on the slopes of Monte Subasio, looks out over the whole countryside. It was here that St. Francis lived and where his spirit is present even today.

Francis, the son of a wealthy cloth merchant, was a fun-loving young man who dreamed about being a soldier who would do great deeds. At that time there were continual feuds between the various cities of Italy, and Assisi was frequently at war with Perugia. During one of the battles, Francis was captured and spent a year in prison. When he returned home, he felt very restless. He didn't really want to be a cloth merchant like his father, and he felt that perhaps he should become a soldier. One day he went into the Church of St. Damian, which was old and badly in need of repairs. As he prayed he seemed to hear a voice saying, "Francis, my house is falling into ruin. Go and repair it for me." Francis rushed home, collected some bales of cloth from his father's warehouse, sold them, and brought the money to the church. However, the priest refused it, saying that Francis had made no sacrifice for it and that what he had done was little better than stealing. This setback really made Francis start to think.

When his father learned that Francis had sold the cloth and tried to give the money away, he was furious. He beat Francis and dragged him to the bishop, shouting that Francis was a thief. The bishop told Francis to return the money. Francis did, but then he stripped off his clothes and handed them to his father. With determination he said, "I give back all that I owe. Up to now, I have called you my father. I do not call you my father any longer. God is now my only Father." His father, now even more angry, gathered up the clothes and the money and stomped off.

Francis put on a rough peasant's robe and went to live among the beggars and the lepers, caring for them as best he could. He decided to rebuild the church with his own hands. He cut rock from the quarry and pulled the stones to the church, building them into walls. At first the townspeople thought that this was another of his crazy antics. Then they came to help him and the church was rebuilt.

Francis came to realize another meaning to the words, "Rebuild my church," when he heard the Gospel passage about the call of the disciples: "Provide yourself with neither gold nor silver nor copper in your belts, no traveling bag, no change of shirt, no sandals, no walking staff. The workman is worth his keep. And as you go, say: 'The kingdom of God is at hand'" (Mt. 10:5ff.).

Suddenly it became clear to Francis what to do. The church is not only constructed from stone but it is built mainly of Christians who profess belief in Jesus Christ. Barefoot and taking nothing with him, he set out to preach about the kingdom of God.

At first Francis preached alone, but soon others joined him. They moved from place to place, helping the poor, comforting the sick and dying, and preaching the word of God. They begged for their food and for shelter at night.

Francis loved all of nature, calling the animals his brothers and sisters. There is a wonderful legend told about him. In the village of Gubbio, the people were terrorized by a wolf that devoured both people and animals.

Since the people never knew when the wolf would come, they were afraid to leave their homes, and they asked Francis for help. Francis went to find the animal, calling: "Brother Wolf, come out." The wolf did, and Francis said to him, "I command you in the name of Jesus not to do harm to anyone." He then took the wolf to the village and told the villagers to feed the wolf every day, convincing them that the wolf had killed only because he was hungry.

After a while, Francis had so many followers that they were no longer able to travel together. Therefore he wrote a rule by which the friars were to live. The men took vows of poverty, chastity, and obedience, but their poverty was of a different kind than that of monks in the monastery. The monk vows poverty, but sometimes the monastery is very rich. For Francis, their poverty had to be absolute. The members were not to store up or lay aside for the future. They were to beg for their needs as they preached.

The way of life which Francis taught was a completely new way of following Christ at that time. Nevertheless, the Pope gave approval to the group in 1210. Called the Friars Minor, they traveled everywhere preaching about Jesus by their life and their words.

Francis traveled as far as the Holy Land. Returning to Italy, he withdrew to a mountain called Alverno to pray and to be in silence. It was there during his prayer that the scars corresponding to Christ's five wounds appeared on his body. This is called the stigmata. They remained on his body and caused pain and weakness until he welcomed "Sister Death" two years later. In art, Francis is often shown with wounds. Most often he is pictured preaching to the birds.

Francis wrote a beautiful hymn called the Canticle (Song) of the Sun, in praise of God the Creator. The name comes from the part where Francis says: "Be praised, my Lord, by all your creatures, above all Brother Sun."

St. Francis was born about 1181 and died in 1226.

His feast day is celebrated on October 4.

St. Francis Xavier

St. Francis Xavier was one of the first followers of St. Ignatius Loyola. He had come from Spain to Paris to study theology. Ignatius had also come from Spain to study theology. Along with a third student they were assigned to the same room. Francis was not very happy about this because he did not like Ignatius' ideas. Ignatius spent a lot of time in prayer, fasting and doing penance. Francis made fun of Ignatius and his talk about bringing people to God, but Ignatius never got angry, and he continued to help him. After a while, the two became very good friends.

When the Society of Jesus was formed and the group had made their center of activity in Rome, the king of Portugal asked for missionaries for India. The Pope told Ignatius to send some members of his Society. Ignatius chose two members for the mission. Francis was not one of them. However, when one of the men chosen for India returned from his mission in Naples, he was very ill, and Ignatius knew that he could not send him. There was no one to send except Francis. The day before the journey was to begin, Ignatius told Francis that he would be one of the missionaries. It was hard for them because they knew that they would probably never see each other again.

Francis Xavier, Simon Rodriguez and Paul of Camerino traveled with the ambassador of India. Francis went to India as the representative of the king of Portugal and also as the ambassador of the Pope. The voyage was difficult beyond imagination. It took them one year and twenty-nine days to reach Goa.

Goa was as large and modern as any city of Europe, with a large cathedral, hospital, schools and even a university. But Francis was appalled at the way the Portuguese rulers treated the people and how little the Christian faith meant to them. One of the missionaries tells how he saw one of the soldiers using his rosary as a counter to be sure that the slaves were getting the right number of lashes.

Portugal was a Christian country. When the king offered protection from the Muslim raiders to the people of southern India, he demanded that the people be baptized and no longer worship idols. About ten thousand people were baptized, but they had received no instruction and did not know anything about the faith they were supposed to profess. Francis left Goa and began work in southern India among the Paravas who were pearl fishermen. He learned to speak a little of the language and had interpreters write the "Our Father," the Apostles' Creed, and the Ten Commandments in the Paravian language.

Francis would go up and down the street ringing a bell, calling the children and others to instruction. When he had a group assembled he would begin by singing the lessons that he had set in rhyme. Then the children would sing them. Afterward he explained the meaning in simple words. Through singing, the prayers and Commandments were learned very quickly. The people loved the singing, and often people walking down the street or a fisherman in his boat could be heard singing the Ten Commandments.

Francis lived like the poor, sharing their food and the huts in which they lived. He cared for the sick and poor, said Mass each week for the lepers, taught and preached.

Francis remained among the Paravas for seven years. His work was often hindered by his assistants who did not have adequate knowledge or ability. In addition, the Paravas were often unwilling to change and the example of many of the Christian Portuguese officials was a scandal. Nevertheless, Xavier had established the beginnings of a living Church. Like everyone else of his time, Xavier did not know very much about the religion of the people whom he came to convert. Therefore, he saw the Moors, the Muslims, and the Buddhists as enemies of God. To him, Christians were right and pagans were wrong—it was as simple as that. He thus destroyed their temples and idols and grew impatient because the people were so slow to change. It was only later, in Japan, that he became aware of the value of the Japanese culture and ancient civilization. Then he no longer destroyed the pagan places of worship but began to use them and give them a Christian purpose. He preached in Ceylon, the Malay Peninsula and the Molucca Islands, returning to Goa from time to time.

In 1549 Francis set out for Japan with two other Jesuits and three Japanese Christians. Japan was such an unknown country that Western explorers were not aware that it consisted of several islands. The missionaries suffered from the cold and lack of food in Japan. The language was difficult to learn, and their interpreter often incorrectly translated the words so that their teaching said exactly the opposite of what they meant. When they preached in the streets, they were scoffed at and often some of the bystanders would pelt them with stones. Barefoot and looking like scarecrows in their ragged clothes, they were turned away from the Buddhist monasteries. Only nobles or rich men bearing gifts for the monks were able to enter into such places.

This gave Francis an idea. If the only way to get to see the prince was by great pomp, then that's what they would do. Through gifts of a friend in Molucca, they obtained fine clothes and gifts for the emperor. In silk kimonos, perhaps with swords in their sashes and colorful turbans, they went to the court, bringing letters from the governor of India and the bishop of India, as well as gifts that were not known in Japan, such as a grandfather's clock, a music box, two pairs of glasses, and crystal vases. The prince gave them permission to teach and decreed that those of his subjects who wanted to become Christians could do so. Francis remained in Japan for two years and organized several communities of Christians there. Then other Jesuits came to replace him.

In 1552, Francis set out for China. At that time foreigners were not allowed to enter that country without permission from the Chinese king. He thus landed on an island and waited for a chance to enter the mainland. However, he became ill and died there within a few weeks. He was alone except for a young Chinese Christian who had come from Goa with him.

We know about his life from the letters he wrote to Ignatius and to the Society of Jesus in Rome. In his writings he only tells about his activities and the places in which he worked. He didn't realize that the letters also showed a life of dedication and zeal, of charity and selflessness, the life of an heroic man dedicated to preaching God's word.

St. Francis Xavier was born in 1506 and died in 1552.
His feast day is celebrated on December 3.

St. Gregory the Great

St. Gregory was born in Rome about the year 540. The son of a Roman senator, he was well educated, a good organizer and a very practical man. When he was about thirty years old, he became prefect of Rome, a very important position in the city. After his father died, Gregory founded six Benedictine monasteries in Sicily and turned his family home in Rome into the Abbey ot St. Andrew. In a short time, he himself entered this monastery.

Gregory was not to remain there for very long, however. Pope Pelagius II asked him to be his ambassador to the emperor of Constantinople. Gregory obeyed and remained in Constantinople for several years. When he returned to Rome, he became the abbot of St. Andrew's and remained an advisor to the Pope. He wanted to remain in the monastery, but when Pope Pelagius died, Gregory was chosen to be his successor.

Gregory was a good Pope, and he led the Church through a time of many difficulties. Rome was under attack by the Lombards, a Germanic tribe who had invaded Italy. When the Lombards were about to attack Rome, Gregory persuaded them to withdraw and tried to make peace with them. Because of these invasions, many people suffered from hunger, sickness and lack of shelter. Gregory organized the property of the Church so that help could be given to the people. Some of the money was used to ransom those whom the Lombards held captive. With the help of the queen of the Lombards, Gregory prepared the way for the conversion of those tribes to the Christian faith.

In 596, Gregory sent Augustine, the prior of St. Andrew's monastery in Rome, and about forty other monks to England to bring the Christian faith to those people. It was unusual at this time for monks to be sent as missionaries. On their arrival in England, the monks contacted King Ethelbert who gave the monks permission to preach in his kingdom. Within a year, the monks had made

many converts, among them King Ethelbert himself. Gregory then sent another missionary team and instructed them to establish churches and to be responsible for various sections of the country.

Gregory was a very wise man. He told the missionaries not to do away with the customs of the people but to change their purpose. The missionaries were not to destroy the pagan temples but rather to put altars in them and make them places of Christian worship. People cannot change their customs all at once; it must be done gradually. The mission to England was the beginning of the Christianization of the entire country.

Gregory was a wise and holy Pope who called himself "The Servant of the Servants of God," a title which all Popes in succeeding years have continued to use. He was a faithful servant of the people of God.

St. Gregory was born about 540 and died in 604.
His feast day is celebrated on September 3.

St. Ignatius Loyola

Have you ever been sick for a long time and had to remain in bed? It wasn't much fun, was it? Often the days seem very long when one is sick.

This happened to St. Ignatius, the youngest of the thirteen children of a noble Spanish family. Born in the family castle of Loyola, he spent his early years as a courtier and then became a soldier in the king's army. In one battle he was wounded in the leg by a cannonball, and since he had to remain in bed for a long until until his leg healed, he asked his friends to find some novels for him to read so that the time would pass more quickly. The only books to be found were one about the life of Christ and another about the lives of the saints.

Ingnatius' conversion began with the reading of these books. After a great deal of thought, he decided to become like Dominic and Francis of Assisi and follow Christ. As soon as he was well enough, he made a pilgrimage to Jerusalem. On the way he went to the shrine of the Blessed Mother at Montserrat and then to a nearby town, Manresa. There he stayed for some months, praying, fasting, and writing down many of his reflections, which later became the Spiritual Exercises. These Exercises are ways of praying and living that help one respond more faithfully to God's love and are practiced by many people even today.

After his pilgrimage to Jerusalem was completed, Ignatius went to several universities in Spain and then to Paris to study theology. He gathered friends around him, men who also wanted to give their lives to the service of the Lord. This group decided to go to Rome and offer to do whatever work Pope Paul III might wish. Before their departure, Ignatius and some of the others were ordained priests.

The Pope asked the group to do many different things: to teach in the university, to preach, to hear confessions, to teach catechism, and to help the sick and the poor. Ignatius gave the Spiritual Exercises to many people.

It was then that the group thought of forming themselves into a society. Ignatius said to his friends, "If anyone asks you who we are, say that we are the Company (Society) of Jesus." Pope Paul III approved the Society in 1540, and Ignatius because its first general.

For the remaining fifteen years of his life,

Ignatius remained in Rome, directing the Society. He saw it grow from ten members to about a thousand. They opened many schools and colleges. The Jesuits, as they were called, went to every country of the world to preach and to teach. Ignatius told his followers that all their work was to be guided by a true love of the Church and obedience to the Pope. This Society, following his directive, has contributed to the renewal of the Church in every age. The motto of the Society of Jesus is: All to the greater glory of God.

St. Ignatius Loyola was born in 1491 and died in 1556.

His feast day is celebrated on July 1.

St. Isaac Jogues and the North American Martyrs

St. Isaac Jogues and his seven companions were the first martyrs of the North American continent.

Isaac was born in Orleans, France. He entered the Society of Jesus, and after his ordination he was sent as a missionary to Canada, assigned to work among the Huron Indians. The Huron tribe was frequently attacked by the Iroquois. During one of these attacks, Isaac and many of the Hurons were captured.

The Iroquois were a savage tribe and they treated their captives in a most cruel way. Isaac and his companions were dragged from village to village. They were beaten and tortured and made to watch their Huron converts being put to death. Isaac finally was ransomed and was able to escape to New York and then to return to his home in France. The Iroquois had cut, chewed or burned off several of his fingers, so he was no longer able to say Mass, but Pope Urban VIII gave him special permission to offer Mass, and that gave him great joy.

After a few months, Isaac and a companion, Jean de Lalande, sailed for the mission among the Hurons and resumed their work. Then he was asked to try to make peace with the Iroquois. He started on this peace mission but he was captured by a Mohawk war party, tomahawked and beheaded. His companion, Jean Lalande, was beheaded the next day.

The first of the missionaries to be martyred was René Goupil, a layman like Lalande, who had offered his services to the missionaries. While a captive, he was killed by an Iroquois who saw him trace the sign of the cross on the forehead of some children. John de Brébeuf (1593–1649) was a French Jesuit who had served among the Indians for many years. He taught the Huron language to all the new missionaries, wrote catechisms, and saw seven thousand Hurons profess their belief in Jesus before his death. He was captured by the Iroquois and suffered a most cruel and inhuman death. Father Gabriel Lalemant (1610–1649) had taken a fourth vow—that of devoting his life to the work of a missionary. He had been in the missions less than three years as an assistant to Father Brébeuf before suffering with him the same dreadful death. Father Anthony Daniel (1601–1648) was also killed by the Iroquois on July 4, 1648. As the Iroquois suddenly attacked the Mission of St. Joseph, Father Anthony baptized as many catechumens as possible. Then he ran to the cabins of the old and sick to baptize them. Going back to the church, he was surrounded by Iroquois, and they shot their arrows into him. Afterward his body was thrown into the chapel which was then set on fire. Father Charles Garnier (1605–1649) was shot to death during an Iroquois attack on the Petun village of St. John, and Father Noel Chabanel (1613–1649) was killed by a Huron who hated Christians.

These martyrs were men of great faith and heroism. They brought the teachings of the Lord Jesus to the primitive Indians of seventeenth-century America. Their only thought was to teach the Indian people about God's love for them, even though they knew that martyrdom would be their reward.

St. Isaac Jogues was born in 1607 and died in 1646.
His feast day is celebrated on October 19.

St. Isidore the Farmer

St. Isidore is the patron saint of farmers and rural communities. He had very little education, and as soon as he was able to use a hoe, he went to work on the farm. He rose early in the morning in order to go to Mass in the village church. All day long, as he walked behind the plow, he prayed. Everything in nature reminded him of the Creator, God our Father.

Known for his love for the poor, Isidore brought them food, prayed with them and encouraged them to remain hopeful. He also had a great concern for animals, taking care to see that they were never mistreated.

Isidore spent his entire life working on a farm at Torrelagune, outside the city of Madrid. He married a young woman who was as simple and holy as he was, and they had one son who died as a child.

Isidore was a kind worker who was honest in his dealings with everyone. His life teaches us the dignity of work, that holiness does not depend upon learning, and that the ordinary actions of the day are the fabric of holiness.

The canonization of Isidore was urged by King Philip III who attributed his recovery from a serious illness to his intercession.

In Spain, Isidore is the patron of the city of Madrid. In the United States, he is the patron of the National Rural Life Conference. In New Mexico, statues of the saint are carried into the fields on his feast day, or whenever there is a lack of rain. The farmers pray that God, through the intercession of St. Isidore, will grant them the blessing of good weather and good crops.

On his feast day, the Church prays: "Lord God, all creation is yours, and you call us to serve you by caring for the gifts that surround us. May the example of St. Isidore urge us to share our food with the hungry and to work for the salvation of mankind."

St. Isidore was born in 1070 and died in 1130.

His feast day is celebrated on May 15.

St. Isidore of Seville

Do you ever use an encyclopedia to find out things that you don't know? An encyclopedia is interesting because it tells about so many different kinds of things.

St. Isidore of Seville was a learned man. In his encyclopedia, called *Etymologiae,* he collected, ordered and summarized all the learning of his time. This work was divided into twenty books and was used as a textbook for hundreds of years.

Isidore was born in Seville, Spain. After the death of his parents, he was educated at a monastery under the direction of his brother, St. Leander. Isidore later entered the monastery and continued his education.

About the year 600, Isidore succeeded his brother as bishop of Seville. That was not an easy job, for Spain had been settled by a Germanic tribe called the Visigoths. The Visigoths were Arians (Christians who said that Christ was not God). The Visigoths and the Catholics were always fighting with each other. Bishop Leander had been a friend of the Visigoth king. When the king became a Catholic, many Arian bishops, nobles and people did the same.

Isidore continued to convert the Visigoths, bringing peace and unity to Spain. He built schools that taught every branch of learning. He wanted Spain to be a center of learning and of culture. It was because of him that Spain had its poets, writers, artists and musicians. Isidore himself wrote seventeen great works on Scripture, theology and history. He was called the most learned man of his time. Through his writings he helped to make known the writings and thoughts of the great teachers before the time of Christ. He also made the works of Augustine, Gregory and the Fathers of the Church known to the people of his time.

Isidore was famous for his learning, for his holiness, and for his generosity to the poor.

St. Isidore was born about 560 and died in 636.

His feast day is celebrated on April 4.

St. Jane Frances de Chantal

Imagine living in a beautiful castle in France, high on a hillside, surrounded only by the sky, trees, and meadows where the cattle stand grazing by the river. This was the home of St. Jane Frances and her husband, Baron Christophe de Rabutin-Chantal. Because Christophe served in the king's army, Jane Frances managed the estates. Very early every morning, all the servants and workers began the day with Mass in the little chapel attached to the house. Then Jane Frances would give the work orders for the day. In the mornings, she would ride her horse to the fields to oversee the work. In the afternoons she took her spinning and worked with the maids.

Jane Frances was especially kind to the poor. Beggars would come to have their bowls filled with the soup that was always on the stove and to receive bread which she often prepared herself. She nursed the sick and cared for neglected old people, showing her love for God in her love for others.

When Christophe came back from the war, their life together was very happy. Then one sad day he was killed in a hunting accident, and suddenly Jane Frances was a widow with three children. She felt very alone and not sure of what to do next. Christophe's father demanded that Jane and the children come to live with him. If she did not come, he would not give the children any of his property or money when he died. In order to provide for the future of her small children, Jane Frances went to his home.

That home was a gloomy place. Her father-in-law was short-tempered and not very pleasant. In addition, the housekeeper, who had been stealing from her employer, was not happy to have Jane Frances there, and she made life as difficult for her as possible. Nevertheless, Jane Frances made the best of it. She gathered all the children on the estate for lessons in reading and counting and she taught them the catechism and their prayers. She also helped the sick and the poor.

During this time Jane Frances met St. Francis de Sales. She had longed for some time to talk to someone about prayer and about the decisions which she felt she must make in her life. She wanted very much to become a nun. Placing herself under the direction of St. Francis, she made two promises: to remain unmarried and to obey his direction.

One day a few years later, Francis de Sales told her of his plan to begin a new religious order for young girls or widows who because of age or health were not able to bear the hardships—long fasts, little sleep, hard manual work—of the older religious orders. The sisters were to divide their time between work and prayer. This order would be different from others in that the sisters would not always remain within the convent. They would go out to visit the poor and nurse the sick.

Jane Frances knew that God was calling her to this work, but she had three children and her father was very old. She spent much time in prayer and became even more sure that God was calling her to this new life. Therefore she asked her father and brother for their permission and help. After they spoke to St. Francis de Sales, they gave permission, and Jane Frances carefully provided for her children, one of whom was already married.

In 1610, Jane Frances and three other women began a new life. Their order was called the Visitation of Holy Mary, and their day was spent in prayer, work, silence, and recreation. Many other women came to join them. Soon under the direction of St. Francis de Sales, she began houses of the Visitation Order in other cities. In Lyon, the archbishop was willing to give permission for a convent to be founded only if the sisters would agree to remain within the convent like the other religious orders and give up their work of visiting the poor and nursing the sick outside the convent. It was a difficult decision, but finally St. Francis de Sales agreed and the Visitation Sisters became an enclosed group.

The Visitation Order grew. St. Francis de Sales directed the sisters until his death in 1622. When Jane Frances died, there were more than eighty convents of Visitation Sisters.

Jane Frances de Chantal lived a life of great faithfulness to God. St. Vincent de Paul said of her: "She was one of the holiest people I have ever met on this earth."

St. Jane Frances de Chantal was born in 1572 and died in 1641.
Her feast day is celebrated on December 12.

St. John Bosco

"What are you looking for?" the priest asked the boy. There was no answer. "Do you want to stay for Mass?" asked the priest. "I've never been to Mass," muttered the boy. "Why don't you stay for Mass, and afterward we can talk?" suggested the priest.

After Mass, Don Bosco learned that the boy's name was Bartholomew Garelli. He was a sixteen-year-old orphan, and, like so many other young boys, he had come to the city of Turin to find work. Such boys lived together, five or six crowded in one room. Often, if they did not find work, they turned to stealing and petty crimes in order to exist.

Don Bosco asked the boy if he would like to learn the catechism, and the boy agreed. The first lesson was right then and there. As Bartholomew was leaving, he said that he intended to come back, and Don Bosco told him that he could bring some of his friends the next time if he wanted to. In a few weeks there were thirty boys. In a few months there were almost a hundred. This incident was the beginning of Don Bosco's life work.

Soon Don Bosco opened a house for these homeless young men. He began workshops for shoemaking, tailoring, and other kinds of work so that the boys could learn a trade. In a short time there were one hundred and fifty young men living at the hospice. After obtaining a printing press, he wrote and printed booklets about the Catholic faith and prayer for the instruction of the young men. Then he began to train others to help him in this work. He admired St. Francis de Sales so greatly that in 1859, when he founded a religious congregation, he called them Salesians. Their work was the education of young boys. In 1872, he founded an order of Salesian sisters to do the same work with young girls.

Don Bosco believed that young people should not be physically punished for their wrongdoing. Rather, they should be placed in a surrounding that would help them to be good. The boys were to be given religious instruction and to be able to receive the sacra-

ments frequently. Their faith was to be the framework in which to live their lives of study, work and play. He insisted that the boys be taught a trade.

Don Bosco believed that learning should be enjoyed. He wrote plays in which the boys could act. He encouraged them to make up entertainments and to play musical instruments. In the fall of the year he would take them into the country. During this holiday period they would help Don Bosco catechize the people of the villages. Don Bosco would preach, hear confessions and celebrate Mass, while the boys would provide entertainment after prayers in the evening for the villagers. The boys used their talents to bring happiness to others.

In later years, the work of the Salesians extended to mission countries. At Don Bosco's death there were over a thousand members in his order and fifty-seven houses in seven countries.

St. John Bosco was born in 1815 and died in 1888.

His feast day is celebrated on January 31.

St. John Nepomucene Neumann

On June 19, 1977, Bishop John Neumann was named a saint of the Catholic Church. It was a day of rejoicing for the whole Church, but in particular for the Church in the United States, for the Redemptorist Congregation, and for the Church in Czechoslovakia, since all three had a role in the making of this saint.

Born in a German-speaking village in Bohemia, John completed his studies for the priesthood at the University of Prague. However, his ordination was delayed because of the bishop's illness and then put off indefinitely because the diocese had enough priests at that time. Therefore John, who had always been interested in being a missionary to America, wrote to several bishops in the United States, and in 1836 he came to this country uncertain as to where he would go.

Bishop Dubois of New York welcomed him gladly, for there were very few priests in the New York area. John was ordained the following year and went to minister among the German immigrants in the Buffalo-Niagara area that encompassed about nine hundred square miles and had only one priest. Life was hard for these poor people. They worked long hours clearing the land, rolling the logs, building their cabins and planting the soil. John traveled from place to place, visiting the sick, the old and the needy, starting catechism classes for the children, and training teachers to continue the instruction. He remained in this area for four years.

John had met some Redemptorist priests and read the biography of their founder, St. Alphonsus Liguori, and he then joined their order. He began his novitiate in 1841 and made his profession of vows in 1842. He was the first Redemptorist to be professed in the United States. During the next few years he served the immigrants in Baltimore and in Pittsburgh. Then he was named the head of the Redemptorist Congregation in the United States.

In 1852 John became the bishop of Philadelphia. As a bishop he did extraordinary work. When he arrived in Philadelphia there were only two schools. Eight years later, there were almost one hundred. He invited many teaching orders of sisters and the Christian Brothers to come to Philadelphia and take charge of the schools. He also built churches and began a preparatory seminary. Despite all these tasks he remained very close to his people. He loved to talk with them, always speaking in their native tongue because he knew at least seven languages. He also made it a practice to conduct several classes for the children and adults whom he would confirm, and he introduced the Forty Hours' Devotion in his diocese, thereby giving the people a special time to pray before the Blessed Sacrament.

Always wanting to help his people, Neumann wrote two catechisms, a Bible history and a handbook for the clergy. The catechisms were written in German for the instruction of the German-speaking immigrants. Bishop Neumann lived the command of the Lord Jesus: "Go and teach all nations." The United States grew in faith and love through the life and teachings of this beloved bishop.

St. John Nepomucene Neumann was born in 1811 and died in 1860.
His feast day is celebrated on January 5.

St. John Vianney—
The Curé of Ars

Ars is a small village in France that has become known all over the world because of one man—St. John Vianney who was the curé (parish priest) of Ars.

When John was a young boy in 1789, there was a great revolution in France. It was a dreadful time, and the people suffered very much. Everyone was poor and there was not enough to eat.

John wanted to be a priest but he had to help his family on the farm. He was not even able to go to school. When he was nineteen, his father said that he could go for instruction to the parish priest in another village and begin his studies to become a priest. However, poor John could hardly read. He went to several seminaries but he failed subject after subject. Finally he was asked to leave the seminary. He went back to the parish priest who again began to teach him. After a few years, the priest asked that John be ordained a priest. He was accepted, not because of his learning but because of his holiness.

Then John was sent to the curé in the village of Ars. The people in the village were not happy to see him because they were no longer living a Christian life, and they did mean things to him in order to get rid of him. Nevertheless, John never stopped preaching to the people and praying for them, and little by little the people began to change. They began to act like Christians again.

The holiness of Father John Vianney soon became known throughout all of France and even outside the country. Thousands of people crowded into Ars to be with him. Soon he was spending almost the entire day in the confessional reconciling people with God and with one another. He said that all men and women have a glorious duty—to pray and to love—and that if they would pray and love, there would be happiness.

The long hours spent hearing confessions took all his strength, but he kept on because

he wanted all people to love God. Called a saint even in his lifetime, he was canonized by Pope Pius XI in 1925 and made the patron of parish priests because of the way in which he served others. By his prayer, good works and holiness of life, he helped the people to know, love and serve the Lord.

St. John Vianney was born in 1786 and died in 1859.

His feast day is celebrated on August 4.

St. Margaret of Scotland

St. Margaret of Scotland lived during a very troubled time. When William the Conqueror sent his armies to conquer England, Margaret, an English princess, and her family fled from England, but they were shipwrecked off the coast of Scotland. The king of Scotland, Malcolm III, befriended them, and in 1070 Margaret married Malcolm. They had six sons and two daughters. Their daughter Matilda later married Henry I of England and was known as Good Queen Maud. Three of the sons, Edgar, Alexander and David, were kings of Scotland. David, one of the best of

the Scottish kings, was honored as a saint by his people.

Margaret took good care of her children, personally teaching them the Christian faith. She managed her own household, and her husband often asked her advice concerning the affairs of his kingdom. In spite of all these duties, Margaret spent time each day in prayer and in reading Scripture. She ate very little and slept only a few hours each night in order to have time for prayer. She was especially kind to the poor and never refused anyone who asked her for help. Margaret did not just give money, but she visited the sick and nursed them herself. Orphans were one of her special concerns.

Margaret was active in the reform of the Church in Scotland. She urged the bishops to try to solve some of the problems, and she made a constant effort to have good priests and teachers in all parts of the country. Through her gifts churches were built and restored, and the monastery at Iona, founded by St. Columban, was rebuilt.

In 1093, the armies of King William Rufus of England made a surprise attack on the castle, and King Malcolm and his son Edward were killed. Margaret was very ill at the time, and on the day that they were killed, she became very sad and said to the nurses, "Perhaps this day a greater evil has come upon Scotland than at any other time." When her son Edgar came back, he did not want to tell his mother about the deaths because she was so very ill, but Margaret just said to him, "I know what happened."

Margaret died four days later and was buried in the church of the Abbey of Dunfermline that she and her husband had founded. It was said of her that every word she uttered and every act she did showed that she was thinking about the things of heaven. Margaret was named a saint of the Church in 1250 and the patroness of Scotland in 1673.

St. Margaret was born about 1045 and died in 1093.

Her feast day is celebrated on November 16.

St. Martin de Porres

St. Martín de Porres, born in Lima, Perú, was the son of a Spanish knight, Don Juan de Porres, and a free black woman from Panama. Don Juan was upset because his children were black like their mother, and he abandoned them for many years. Later he came back for them, only to abandon them again.

When Martín was about twelve, his mother sent him to learn how to be a barber-surgeon. In those days, the job of a barber was linked to medicine. Martín learned how to cut hair, draw blood (a common medical treatment for fever), care for wounds, and prepare and apply medicines. He used his knowledge to take care of the sick, especially among the poor.

Soon Martín had many people coming to him for help and he had no time for prayer. Finally, he decided to join the Third Order of Dominicans in Lima. He asked to be admitted as a servant and to be given the most menial tasks to do. He served the community by working on the farm, cleaning the stable, tending the garden, doing the laundry, and cleaning the house. He spent many hours in prayer, most of them at night because he had so many jobs to do during the day.

Because Martín was black, he often had to endure many insults. Some of the friars thought that he had no right to be a part of their community. However, he remained gentle and kind, turning to our Lord in prayer. Finally, he was asked to take charge of the infirmary. He was kind to the sick and very skillful in healing them. He would sit with the patients at night to comfort them and to pray with them.

All of the friars came to respect Martín because of his holiness. Some of them even asked him to direct them in their prayer.

The people of the town, poor and rich alike, began to come to Martín with their illnesses and ailments. So many people came that Martín finally had to turn some houses into hospitals in order to care for them. These houses quickly became overcrowded.

One day a woman stopped Martín on the street, and before he realized what was happening, she thrust a tiny baby into his hands, begging him to take care of it. Martín took the baby to his sister's house. The news spread quickly, and soon many babies were brought to him. The people were so poor that they were unable to buy food or clothing for their children.

Martín begged for money in order to build a home for these infants. He also was given land on which the poor could grow food, and rich people helped him with gifts of money. He influenced all the people of Lima because he was an example of a life given completely to God and of selfless service to the sick and poor.

One evening Martín himself became sick. He told the friar not to waste any medicine on him because he was going to die. The Dominican friars gathered around his bed to

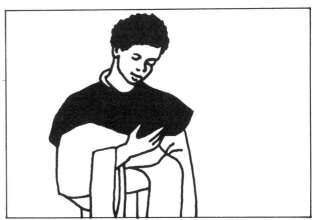

say the prayers for the dying, and Martín used what little strength he had to ask pardon for any bad example he had given. Then he died. The whole city of Lima was filled with sorrow when the people learned of his death.

When he was canonized in 1962, Pope John XXIII described the generosity of his life when he said, "Common people responded to him by calling him 'Martín the charitable.'" What a wonderful way to be known!

St. Martín de Porres was born in 1579 and died in 1639.

His feast day is celebrated on November 3.

St. Monica

Most of what we know about the life of St. Monica is told to us by her son, St. Augustine, in his famous book, *Confessions*.

Monica was born about the year 331 in North Africa. Her parents gave her in marriage to Patricius who was not a Christian. Life with Patricius was not easy, for he had a bad temper, was not dependable, and made fun of Monica's prayers and Christian practices. Nevertheless Monica remained faithful and loving to him. As a result, Patricius finally gave up his bad ways of acting, and before his death he became a Christian.

Augustine, the oldest of their three children, was about seventeen years old when Patricius died. He was a great source of worry for his mother, since he seemed restless and only interested in his own pleasure. It was the custom at that time not to baptize infants but rather to teach the children the Christian beliefs and way of life before they were baptized. Monica prayed with all her heart that Augustine would choose to be baptized. However, he seemed to have given up any Christian practices he might have had. He joined a group that believed false teachings and preached against the Catholic faith. Monica told him that she would not allow him to eat or sleep at her house until he changed his ways. Later, she realized that turning him away would not help him, for people only change when they are loved.

After that, Monica stayed close to Augustine—in fact, sometimes too close for Augustine's comfort. When he made plans to go to Rome to teach, she was determined to go with him. However, he tricked her by telling her that he was going to the docks to say goodbye to a friend. Instead he himself got on the boat and sailed for Rome. But Monica was not one to give up. She followed Augustine to Rome only to discover that he had gone on to Milan. At that time, travel was mostly by walking, so it was a long and difficult trip.

In Milan Monica learned that Augustine had met Bishop Ambrose and was preparing

to become a Catholic. That news made her very happy, for she loved her son very much and wanted him to be all that God had called him to be. Therefore she thanked God over and over.

After Augustine was baptized, Monica and Augustine planned to return to Africa. While waiting for a boat the seaport of Ostia, she became very sick. However, she told Augustine that the one thing she had lived for had been to see him become a Catholic. Now she was ready to die. She asked Augustine to do only one thing for her: to remember her at the altar of the Lord wherever he would be.

Monica's love for her son is like the love of the forgiving father in the story of the prodigal son in the Gospel. It reminds us again of the love that God has for each of us.

St. Monica was born about 331 and died in 387.
Her feast day is celebrated on August 27.

St. Patrick

When St. Patrick was sixteen years old, he was kidnapped by pirates and taken as a slave to Ireland. Although his parents were Catholics, the religion of his parents had not interested him. However, when he was a slave, he came to know and to love God very much. In an account of his life called *Confessio*, Patrick wrote: "But after I came to Ireland . . . every day I had to tend sheep, and many times a day I prayed . . . and the love of God came to me more and more, and my faith grew stronger."

After six years of slavery, Patrick escaped and was able to return to his home. While he was back with his parents, it is said that he had a dream calling him back to Ireland to preach Christ to the Irish people. In that dream a man brought him many letters. Patrick took one of the letters and began to read. The opening words of the letter were: "The voices of the Irish cry out: 'Come and walk with us once more.' " Patrick tells that he became so sad that he woke up. He took this dream to be a sign that he must go back to Ireland, and he was ordained a priest.

Because Patrick did not have much schooling, his superiors did not want to send him to Ireland. However, when Palladius, the first bishop of Ireland died, Patrick was sent to take his place. He preached especially in the north and west of Ireland where the Gospel had not been preached before. He made friends with the local kings and they allowed him to preach Christ to the people, many of whom became Christians.

Patrick was often in danger; at times he even faced death. The Druids did not want the people to become Christians. These Druids, who were thought to be magicians and wizards, knew that they would not have power over the people if the people were converted, so they tried to stop him from telling the people about Christ.

Nevertheless, in spite of the danger Patrick continued to preach and to build churches. The people continued to become Christians and gradually Christianity spread throughout Ireland. Today the Irish people both in Ireland and throughout the world look upon Patrick as their patron saint and honor him for bringing the faith to Ireland.

When we see a statue or picture of St. Patrick, we often see him holding a shamrock. The story was told that one day when Patrick was preaching to the people about the Holy Trinity—the Father, Son and Holy Spirit—he picked a shamrock from the ground and used it to explain to the people about the three persons in one God. Just as there are three leaves on the one stem which make up one shamrock, so too there are three persons but only one God.

Patrick's whole life was devoted to praising and serving God. A beautiful morning prayer, called "The Breastplate of St. Patrick," was written after St. Patrick died, but it was a prayer of praise such as St. Patrick might have said.

I bind unto myself today
The power of God to hold and lead.
His eye to watch, his might to stay,
His ear to listen to my need,
The wisdom of my God to teach.
His hand to guide, his shield to protect,
The word of God to give me speech,
His heavenly messengers to be my guard.

Christ be with me, Christ within me,
Christ behind me, Christ before me,
Christ beside me, Christ to win me,
Christ to comfort and restore me,
Christ beneath me, Christ above me,
Christ in quiet, Christ in danger,
Christ in the hearts of all who love me,
Christ in the mouth of friend or stranger.

I bind unto myself the name,
The strong name, of the Trinity
By calling on the same,
The Three in One, the One in Three,
From whom all nature has creation:
Eternal Father, Spirit, Word.
Praise to the Lord of my salvation.
Salvation is of Christ the Lord. Amen.

St. Patrick was born about the year 390 and died about 461.

His feast day is celebrated on March 17.

St. Rose of Lima

Do your family and friends call you by a nickname? St. Rose of Lima was baptized Isabel de Flores y del Oliva, but as a tiny baby she was nicknamed Rosa or Rosita, and this was the name by which she was known for the rest of her life.

Rose was one of the oldest of the many children in her family. She worked hard to help her mother care for the other children. She grew flowers and did embroidery and other needlework to sell in order to help support the family.

Rose's mother wanted her to marry someone who was wealthy, but Rose did not want to marry at all. She knew that God wanted her to do something else. Her wish was to join a convent where she could spend the whole day in prayer. Her parents objected because they needed the money that she earned from selling her needlework and flowers. As a result Rose then joined the Third Order of St. Dominic. Although she wore the Dominican habit, she lived at home and did all her usual work.

Rose felt that God wanted her to live a life of penance, and she would offer such acts of penance for those who did not believe in God or who did not love him. For example, under her veil she wore a silver band with points on the inside that dug into her head. She did this in memory of the crown of thorns that pierced Our Lord's head. She had only bread and water for food and lived alone in a tiny hut behind the house of her parents, spending many hours of the day and night in prayer.

Rose also knew that our love for God is shown by our love for others. Therefore she used a room in the home of her parents to nurse the poor who were sick. Many people came to Rose for help, and she never turned anyone away. However, because of the hard life of penance she led, she soon became very sick herself and did not recover.

Many people knew of Rose's holiness, and when she died, the decision was made not to have a Mass for the dead but to have a celebration in honor of all the saints. The people wanted to see Rose once more, to touch her and to bring the sick where they could see her. Each day, for several days, the funeral could not take place because of the great crowds of people who came to view her body. Finally Rose was buried privately in the Dominican church.

About fifty years after her death, Pope Clement X named Rose a saint of the Church. She was also named patron of all of South America and of the Philippine Islands.

St. Rose of Lima was born in 1586 and died in 1617.
Her feast day is celebrated on August 23.

St. Teresa of Avila

As a little girl, St. Teresa of Avila was determined to be a saint. Having read many stories of the saints, she persuaded her brother to run away with her to a pagan place. There, she explained, they would probably be beheaded because they believed in Christ, and then they would be martyrs. Fortunately the children were found before they had gotten very far and were brought back home.

When Teresa was ten, her mother died and she became very lonely and sad. Her father sent her to be cared for at a convent school. There Teresa wondered if God was calling her to be a nun.

When she was twenty years old, Teresa decided to enter the Carmelite Convent of the Incarnation in Avila. A short time later she had to return home because of sickness, but after a few years she returned to the convent.

Life in that convent was not very strict. The sisters could use their own property and money, and they did not observe the laws of fasting or the rule of silence. In fact, they spent a lot of time visiting with their friends from the town. Teresa did the same thing, even neglecting prayer at times. Gradually, however, she realized that Our Lord wanted her to live differently and to begin a convent where the sisters would follow the original Carmelite rule of prayer, poverty, silence and fasting.

Teresa planned to use a house in the city of Avila for the new convent, but both the sisters in the Convent of the Incarnation and the townspeople were against the idea. "Why have another convent?" they asked. The townspeople thought it would cost them money, and the sisters did not like to be told that they were living in a lax way. There was a lot of trouble for a while but eventually the problems were resolved.

Teresa and four others began the new house. Their life was very strict. They spent many hours in prayer, kept almost complete silence and never ate meat. They had had no income but lived on alms, and wore clothing of the coarsest material and sandals instead of shoes. About five years later, Teresa was asked to begin similar convents in other cities. She did this for the next twenty years. It was hard work because of the opposition, misunderstanding and criticism that came from many people, both within and outside the Carmelite Order. However, under her influence, the reform spread even to the men of the Order. St. John of the Cross later took charge of these houses and opened new ones in other cities.

During the years that she founded many new convents, Teresa also wrote many books in obedience to the request of her spiritual director. One was the story of her life. Another, called *The Way of Perfection,* was written for the direction of her nuns. Still another, *The Book of Foundations,* told the story of the beginnings of the convents which she had founded, while *The Interior Castle* tells of the way of prayer. These books are read by many people even today.

Teresa was named a Doctor of the Church in 1970. She and St. Catherine of Siena are the only two women to be given this honor. A Doctor of the Church is distinguished by faithfulness to Church teaching, personal holiness and learning. St. Ambrose, St. Jerome, St. Augustine, St. Gregory the Great and about thirty others have this title.

St. Teresa lived a life of great activity and yet one of deep prayer. It was the awareness of God's love for her that helped her to go on in spite of opposition, difficulties in prayer, sickness and misunderstanding. Her faithfulness and trust in God's love showed that she loved the Lord God with her whole heart.

St. Teresa was born in 1515 and died in 1582.

Her feast day is celebrated on October 15.

St. Thérèse
of the Child Jesus

Sometimes it is easy to imagine that a person can become a saint only by doing great, extraordinary actions. St. Thérèse of Lisieux teaches us that holiness comes about by doing little things well.

When Thérèse was fifteen years old, she became a Carmelite nun in Lisieux, France. Two of her sisters were already members of that community of sisters. Thérèse did nothing extraordinary during the day, but whatever she did, she did as well as she could. She scrubbed the floors, set the table, washed the clothes and even accepted corrections when she did not deserve them. These were little things, but Thérèse made all of them a prayer. She remembered that as a small child, she used to pick flowers to bring to her mother and father to show them that she loved them. Thérèse compared her everyday actions to these flowers. She brought her everyday actions to God to show that she loved him. For this reason, St. Thérèse is often called "The Little Flower."

After a few years, Thérèse was appointed to be the mistress of novices. Novices were those women who were preparing to become Carmelite sisters. Thérèse helped them to pray and to grow in holiness. During this time her sister, Celine, joined the community.

Thérèse had never been blessed with very good health, and finally she became seriously ill with a lung disease. When she died, she was just twenty-four years old and had been a nun for only nine years.

Shortly before her death, Sister Thérèse was asked to write her memories of her childhood and then to add a section telling about her "little way" of loving God. After Thérèse's death, this book was read by many people. In it she showed that it was possible to be a saint simply by doing little things well out of love for God. Many people turned to her in prayer, and soon miracles and answers to prayer came about through her intercession. St. Thérèse prays for us now. Before her death she said, "I will spend my heaven in doing good upon earth."

St. Thérèse of Lisieux was born in 1873 and died in 1897.
Her feast day is celebrated on October 1.

St. Thomas Aquinas

St. Thomas Aquinas was one of the greatest teachers of all time. Born at Roccasecca near the Benedictine Abbey of Monte Cassino in Italy, his father was the Count of Aquino. After his fifth birthday, Thomas was sent to school at the Abbey of Monte Cassino. His family hoped that he would choose the Benedictine way of life and perhaps someday even become the abbot of the great monastery.

At that time there was a great struggle going on between the Pope and Emperor Frederick II. When Frederick sent troops to occupy Monte Cassino as a fortress, the monks, of course, were put out of the abbey, and Thomas was sent to Naples to study. While at the University of Naples, Thomas joined the Dominicans. His family was very upset by his decision. They considered it unthinkable that their son of noble birth should join a group that had no monasteries or wealth and that begged for their food.

When the Dominicans sent Thomas to Paris for his novitiate, his mother sent a message to her oldest son, Rinaldo, to bring Thomas back. Rinaldo did and Thomas was forced to stay at home. However, after some time his mother realized that she could not make him change his mind. He then went to Paris and later to Cologne in Germany to study with St. Albert the Great. The rest of his life was given to teaching, preaching, study and especially to writing.

Thomas was a brilliant student. His memory and his power to concentrate were extraordinary, and supposedly he never forgot anything that he read. Students who wrote while Thomas dictated said that he could dictate to three or even four secretaries on different subjects at the same time. His writings have influenced and still influence the theologians in the Church. It was said of him that his wonderful learning was due more to the depth of his prayer than to his own genius.

Thomas taught at several of the great universities of the time. He was also in charge of the house of studies for the Dominican Order in Rome. Many works were written by Thomas during these years. He had the great gift of being able to organize and to write clearly. The *Summa Theologica*, his last and greatest work, gives a magnificent summary of Catholic theology.

Pope Gregory X asked Thomas to come to a Church council at Lyons, but he died on the way there. His whole life had been devoted to the search for and the defense of truth. The truths which Thomas wrote about were the realities by which he lived.

St. Thomas Aquinas was born about 1225 and died in 1274.
His feast day is celebrated on January 28.

St. Thomas More

Many people think that you cannot live like ordinary people and be a saint. They think saints spend all their time doing "holy" things or that they have to go to live in the desert or in a monastery.

St. Thomas More didn't seem to do "holy" things. He was a most cheerful man who enjoyed having friends visit him in his house in Chelsea, just outside London. He had lots of friends who came from many countries to stay with him. He used to say "Praise God and be merry" and he loved to be at home with his family. He was a very important man because he was the Lord Chancellor of England, the man with the most power after the king.

Thomas had to travel a lot in France and Germany, but he always wrote home to his wife and to his children whom he loved very much indeed. He began one letter with the words: "Thomas More to his whole School." His family was a large one because it included his wife and his four children and foster children and their husbands and wives, and it must have seemed like a school.

Thomas was a very learned man who believed in the rebirth of learning that was then sweeping through Europe. One of his greatest friends was Erasmus who wrote that while most people thought that women should not bother their heads with studies, Thomas taught all his children, boys and girls alike. In fact, Margaret, the eldest, was one of the best educated.

Thomas was a lawyer. His father had been a judge, and he sent him to Oxford and to London to study. For a while Thomas thought that he might become a monk, and he spent four years with the Charterhouse monks. Finally he came to realize that most of all he would like to be married with a family, so he left the monastery and settled in Chelsea. He was one of the most brilliant lawyers in all Europe and was named a judge at the age of thirty-three. He was a very popular judge, especially among the poorer people, because he was always fair in his decisions. He was also quick at coming to those decisions so that the people did not have to wait a long time for justice.

When King Henry VIII made Thomas his Lord Chancellor in 1529, Thomas was unhappy at having to spend so much time at court. He never thought that all the outward display of learning, wealth, or power was what really mattered, though he had all of these things himself. He saw that there was a lot of dishonesty in the court, and his friend Erasmus told him that he ought not to have anything to do with politics for this reason. But Thomas wrote back, "If you cannot deal with vices as you would like to do, by getting people to stop them altogether, that is no reason for turning your back on them; you must handle everything as gently as you can, and what you cannot put right, you must try to make as little wrong as possible."

King Henry wanted to make himself the head of the Church so that he could decide for himself what was right and what was wrong. Thomas could have agreed with him and remained the Lord Chancellor, but he thought that the king was doing wrong. If he had stayed as Lord Chancellor, it would have been the same thing as saying that he agreed with the king, so he resigned. The king tried to make Thomas agree with him, promising him all sorts of rewards if he would agree, but Thomas could not do that. And so he was put into the Tower of London, which was a famous prison in those days. Thomas' friends tried to get him to agree with the king so that he could be free and enjoy his own family and house, but he answered: "Is not this house (by which he meant his prison) as near heaven as my own?"

Therefore the king ordered Thomas to be beheaded. Just before he died he said to the onlookers, "I die the king's good servant, but God's first."

St. Thomas More was born in 1478 and died in 1535.
His feast day is celebrated on June 22.